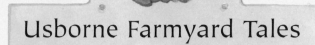
Usborne Farmyard Tales

Things to make and do

Anna Milbourne

Designed by Non Figg and Amanda Gulliver
Illustrated by Stephen Cartwright
and Molly Sage

Photographs by Howard Allman

Contents

There is a little yellow duck for you to find on every double page.

This is Apple Tree Farm.

Mr. and Mrs. Boot live here with their
two children, Poppy and Sam. They
have a dog called Rusty and a cat
called Whiskers. Ted drives the tractor
and helps out on the farm.

Poppy's paper daisy chains

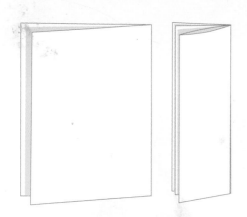

Make all the stems go off the sides of the paper.

1. Fold a rectangle of white paper in half so that the two shorter edges meet. Then fold it in half again.

2. Draw a daisy near the top of the folded paper. Add a thick stem on each side. Draw two more daisies underneath.

3. Using a pair of scissors, cut around the daisies, but don't cut along the folds at the ends of the stems.

4. Open out your daisy chains. Use a yellow felt-tip pen to add the middles of the daisies.

Add the edges of the petals before you fill in the stems.

5. Fill in the stems using a green felt-tip pen. Then tape your daisy chains together to make one long chain.

Hand-print crow

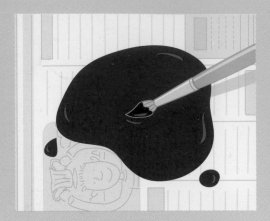

1. Pour some black paint onto an old newspaper. Spread the paint out with a paintbrush.

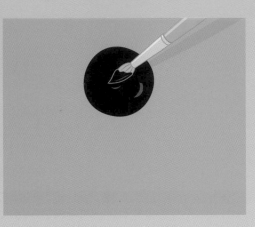

2. Paint a crow's round head near the top of a big piece of paper. Make it almost as wide as your hand.

3. Dip your brush into the black paint again and paint a big, fat body underneath the crow's head.

Make sure the wing is touching the body.

4. Turn your picture upside down. Dip your hand into the paint and press it onto the paper to print a wing.

5. Dip your other hand into the paint. Press it down on the other side of the body to print another wing.

6. Wash your hands. Then pour a little orange paint and a little white paint onto some more old newspaper.

Turn your crow back the right way around.

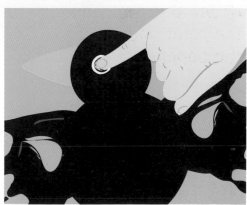

7. Dip a clean brush into the orange paint and paint a beak on your crow. Add his legs and feet too.

8. Dip the tip of your finger into the white paint. Press it onto the crow's head to make an eye. Let it dry.

9. Dip the tip of your little finger into the black paint. Press it in the middle of the white circle.

5

Finger-puppet mice

1. Place a mug on top of a piece of white paper. Draw around it to make a circle. Then cut the circle out.

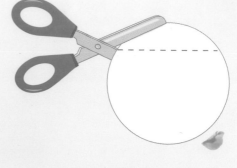

2. Cut a piece the width of two of your fingers off the circle to make a straight edge, like this.

3. Spread glue halfway along the straight edge, and then bend it around to make a cone. Hold it until it sticks.

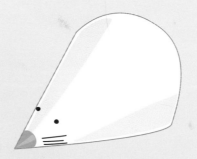

4. Using felt-tip pens, draw a pink nose, black whiskers and two little black eyes on the cone's pointed end.

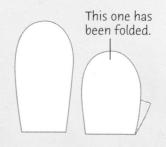

This one has been folded.

5. Cut two long ear shapes out of the piece of paper you cut off the circle. Fold their ends over, like this.

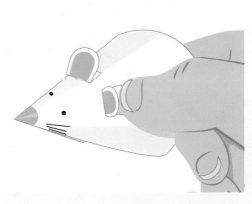

6. Fill in the middles of the ears with pink felt-tip pen. Spread glue under the folds and press them onto the cone.

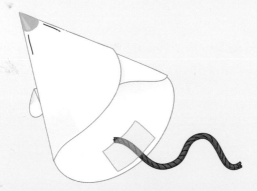

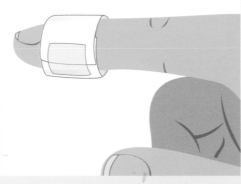

Leave your puppet to dry before you use it.

7. Cut a piece of string for the mouse's tail. Lay the mouse on its back and tape the tail inside the cone.

8. Cut a thin strip of paper and wrap it around your finger. Press a piece of tape on to hold it in place.

9. Put a blob of glue on the rolled-up piece of paper and press it inside the mouse puppet, like this.

Sam's froggy door sign

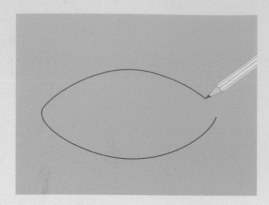

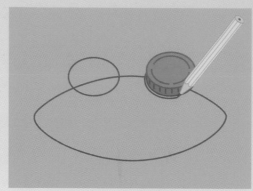

Use the side without pencil marks as the front of the frog's head.

1. Draw a big leaf shape for the frog's head on a piece of green paper. Make the leaf shape about as wide as this page.

2. Draw around a small jar lid to make two big eye shapes on top of his head. Then carefully cut around your frog's head.

3. Cut a big round shape for the body. It doesn't have to be perfectly round. Make it a little narrower than the head.

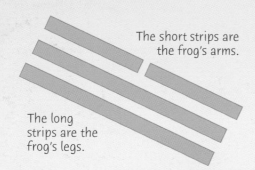

The short strips are the frog's arms.

The long strips are the frog's legs.

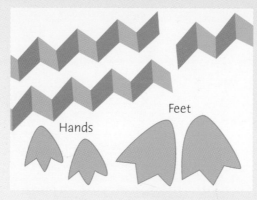

Hands

Feet

This is the back of the frog.

4. Cut three long strips of paper, each about as long as this page. Fold one strip in half. Cut along the fold to make two shorter strips.

5. Fold each strip lots of times to make zigzags. Draw two hands and two feet on a piece of green paper and cut them out.

6. Tape the head onto the body. Then tape the arms and legs onto the body. Tape the hands and feet onto the arms and legs.

These will be the frog's eyes.

7. Put a small jar lid on a piece of white paper. Draw around it to make two circles. Fill in their middles with a felt-tip pen. Cut them out.

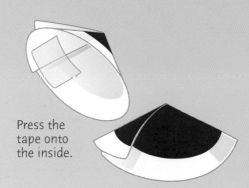

Press the tape onto the inside.

8. Snip into the middle of each circle. Pull the cut edges in so they overlap, making a shallow cone, and tape them in place.

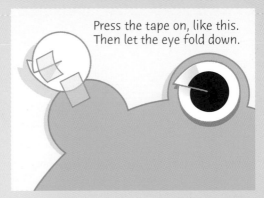

Press the tape on, like this. Then let the eye fold down.

9. Cut another piece of tape. Press one end inside a cone eye, and the other end onto the frog's head. Tape the other eye on like this too.

10. Using a black felt-tip pen, draw nostrils and a big smile on your frog. Write your name on its tummy and hang it on your bedroom door.

Sam's room

If you want your frog to have a pale tummy like this one, glue it on before you tape on the frog's head.

Snail-trail letter paper

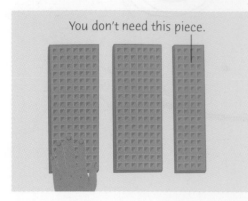

You don't need this piece.

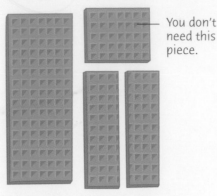

You don't need this piece.

Bend the bottom strip over the top ones to start rolling them up.

1. Cut two strips off a piece of sponge cloth. Make each strip about the same width as your hand.

2. Trim about a third off the top of one of the strips. Then cut the strip in half lengthways.

3. Lay the two small strips on top of the big one, with a gap at each end. Then start rolling them up, like this.

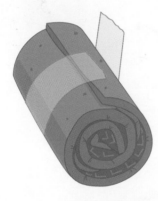

Rinse your spoon between spreading the two different paints.

Make sure there isn't too much paint on your roll.

4. Roll the strips all the way up. Then cut a piece of tape and wrap it around the roll to hold it in place.

5. Pour a little red and a little yellow paint onto an old plate. Spread the paint out with an old spoon.

6. Dip one end of the roll into the yellow paint. Press it onto a piece of paper to print a snail shell.

Dear Alice,
Please come to play on Friday after school.
Love from Poppy

Dear Ted,
Thank you for my lovely birthday present.
Love, Sam

Please come to my birthday party on May 2nd at 3pm at Apple Tree Farm.
Poppy

Once your snail paper is dry, you can use it for writing letters or invitations.

To print a snail facing the other way, use the other end of your sponge roll.

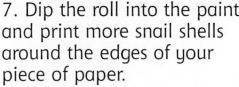

7. Dip the roll into the paint and print more snail shells around the edges of your piece of paper.

8. Dip your finger into the red paint. Finger paint a curvy snail's body. Add the other snails' bodies too.

9. When the snails are dry, use a felt-tip pen to draw their eyes and mouths. Add feelers on their heads.

If you don't have glitter glue, use normal glue and sprinkle glitter onto it.

10. Squeeze a wavy line of glitter glue leading from the back of each snail. These are their shiny trails.

Leaf-print butterflies

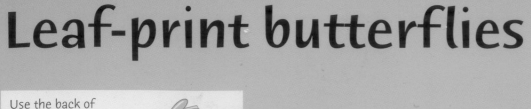

Use the back of the spoon.

1. Put a piece of sponge cloth on top of an old newspaper. Pour a little paint on top. Spread it out with an old spoon.

Leaves with veins that stick out make good prints.

2. Press a leaf onto the sponge cloth, with the veins facing down. Then press it onto a piece of paper and peel it off to make a print.

3. Make three more leaf prints on the same piece of paper. Leave them to dry. Then carefully cut around them.

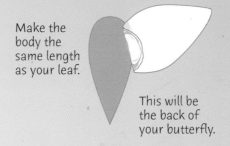

Make the body the same length as your leaf.

This will be the back of your butterfly.

4. Cut a long shape for the butterfly's body from bright paper. Put a blob of glue on the front of a leaf print and press it onto the body.

5. Glue the other three leaf shapes onto the body, like this, so they look like butterfly wings. Leave the glue to dry.

These butterflies have been decorated with sequins.

You can use stickers from the sticker pages to decorate your butterflies.

These are the feelers.

6. Cut two thin strips of paper as long as your finger. Roll up the ends to make them curl. Then tape them onto the back of the head.

7. Turn your butterfly over. Use a felt-tip pen to draw its mouth and eyes. Then decorate its wings with glitter glue or shiny stickers.

13

Growing shoots

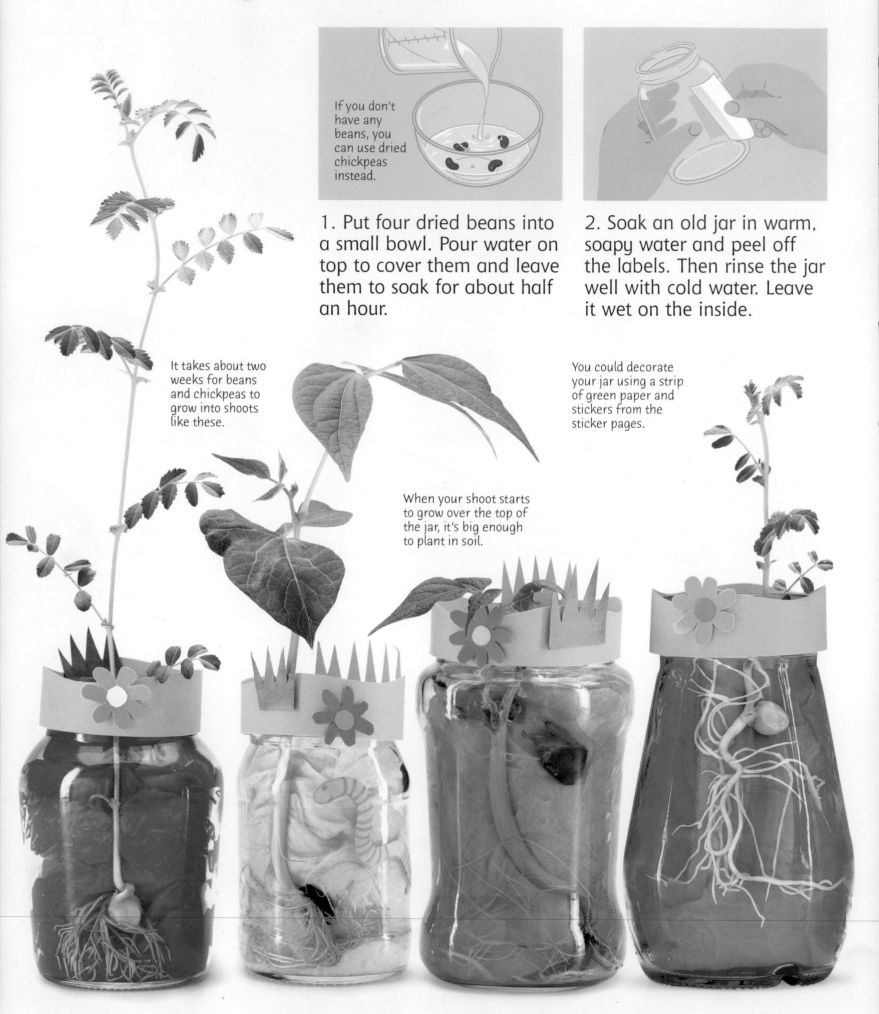

If you don't have any beans, you can use dried chickpeas instead.

1. Put four dried beans into a small bowl. Pour water on top to cover them and leave them to soak for about half an hour.

2. Soak an old jar in warm, soapy water and peel off the labels. Then rinse the jar well with cold water. Leave it wet on the inside.

It takes about two weeks for beans and chickpeas to grow into shoots like these.

You could decorate your jar using a strip of green paper and stickers from the sticker pages.

When your shoot starts to grow over the top of the jar, it's big enough to plant in soil.

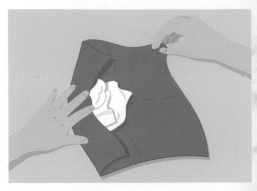

3. Scrunch up a paper towel. Open out a bright paper napkin and wrap it around the scrunched-up paper towel to make a bundle.

4. Push the bundle into the jar. Hold the napkin away from the side of the jar and push a bean down between the jar and the napkin.

5. Push the other three beans between the napkin and the side of the jar. Then press the napkin back to hold them in place.

A sunny window sill is a good place to grow your beans.

6. Use a big spoon to add water to the jar, making sure the napkin gets fairly wet. Then put the jar in a warm, bright place.

Planting your shoot

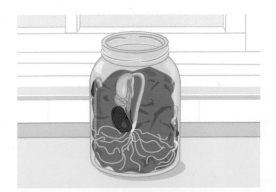

7. Spoon more water into the jar every day, to keep the napkin wet. After two or three days, shoots will begin to grow.

Make the dip big enough to hold your shoot's roots.

1. Put some small stones into a plant pot with a hole in it. Fill the pot almost to the top with compost. Make a dip in the compost.

Let the roots sit in the dip.

2. Carefully lift a shoot out of the jar. Hold it upright in the pot and add compost around it. Press the compost down. Water the shoot every few days.

Piggy picture frame

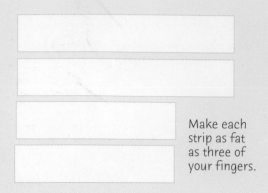

Make each strip as fat as three of your fingers.

1. Cut two strips of thick yellow paper about the length of this page and two more strips about the width of this page.

2. Spread glue on both ends of one of the short strips. Press the long strips onto it. Glue on the other short strip to make a frame.

You can tape a picture to the back of the frame.

If you don't have pink paint, mix some white and red paint together.

3. Pour a little pink paint onto a plate. Dip your finger into the paint. Press it onto the frame to print a pig's body. Print lots more.

4. Let the paint dry. Then use a black felt-tip pen to draw the pigs' eyes, ears and snouts. Add their legs and give them each a curly tail.

Pussycat bookmark

1. On a piece of thick white paper, draw a cat's head and two paws, like this. Fill them in with felt-tip pens.

2. Cut around the shape. Then put it on top of another piece of thick paper and draw around it using a pencil.

You don't need to fill in this part.

3. Add a cat's body under the pencil outline and fill it in with felt-tip pens. Cut around the whole cat shape.

4. Spread glue on the top part of the head. Then press the filled-in head shape on top, lining up the ears.

Leave your bookmark to dry before you use it.

Hook the cat's paws over a page to mark your place in a book.

Dangly scarecrow

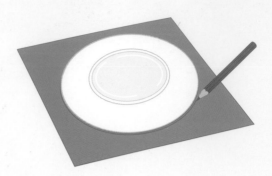

Keep the other semicircle to use later.

1. Put a plate onto a piece of thick blue paper. Draw around it using a pencil. Then cut out the circle.

2. Fold the circle in half and then open it out again. Cut along the fold to make two semicircles.

3. Spread some glue about halfway along the flat edge of one of the semicircles, like this.

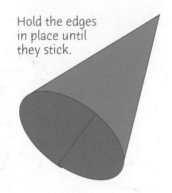

Hold the edges in place until they stick.

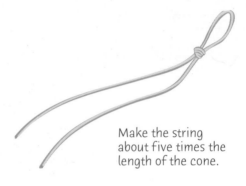

Make the string about five times the length of the cone.

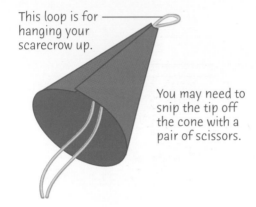

This loop is for hanging your scarecrow up.

You may need to snip the tip off the cone with a pair of scissors.

4. Holding the straight edge, bend the semicircle around to make a cone. Press the edges together.

5. Cut a long piece of string. Fold it in half. Then tie a knot near the folded end to make a loop.

6. Push the string up through the cone, so that the loop pokes out of the top and the knot is inside.

Draw little lines around his nose so that it looks stitched on.

7. Draw a scarecrow's face on a piece of thick white paper. Add a hat and hair. Fill them in. Then cut it out.

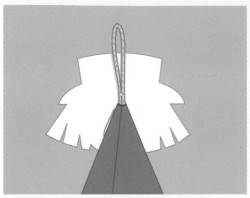

8. Put a blob of glue on the back of the scarecrow's head. Press the head onto the cone body.

This will make two shoes.

9. Fold the leftover blue semicircle in half. Draw a shoe shape. Then cut it out through both layers of paper.

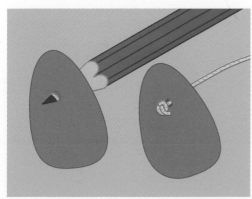

10. Using a pencil, poke a hole in each shoe. Push the string through the shoe and tie a knot in the bottom.

You could make a crow too. To make a smaller cone, use a cup instead of a plate to draw the circle.

This crow's eyes, beak and wings were cut out and stuck on.

You could draw pockets and buttons on the scarecrow's coat.

Fingerprint sheep card

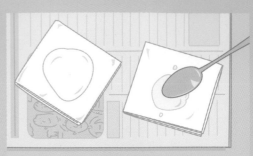

Rinse the spoon so you don't mix the paints.

1. To make a card, fold a piece of thick yellow paper in half so that the two shorter edges meet. Press along the fold.

2. Cut a rectangle of green paper, a little smaller than your card. Spread glue on the back and then press it onto the front of your card.

3. Put two paper towels on top of an old newspaper. Pour a little white and yellow paint on top. Spread the paint out with a spoon.

4. Dip the tip of your finger into the white paint. Press it onto the card to make a fingerprint. Add lots more to make a sheep's body.

5. Dip your thumb into the paint. Make a thumbprint for the sheep's face. Add some more fingerprints on top of the sheep's head.

6. Once the paint is dry, use a black felt-tip pen to draw two dots for the sheep's eyes. Then add its nose, ears and legs.

7. Dip your finger into the yellow paint to make little fingerprinted flowers on the grass. Add white fingerprints for their middles.

Here are a few more ideas for different sheep cards you can make.

Write a message inside your card. You could use it as a birthday or Easter card.

Bright bug giftwrap

You will need this piece later.

1. Put a paper towel on top of an old newspaper. Pour red paint on top and spread it out with the back of an old spoon.

2. Cut a small potato in half. Push a fork into one half to use as a handle. Cut the end off the other half of the potato.

3. Dip the half potato into the red paint. Press it onto a big piece of paper to print a bug body. Print lots more bugs in the same way.

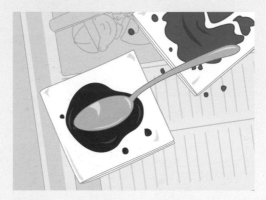

This will be the bug's head.

4. Put another paper towel on top of the newspaper. Pour a little black paint on top and spread it out with a spoon.

5. Push the fork into the cut-off piece of potato. Dip it into the black paint and press it onto each of the bugs' bodies.

6. Dip the tip of your finger into the black paint. Press it onto a bug's back to print a spot. Fingerprint lots more spots on all of the bugs.

7. Wash your hands and let the bugs dry. Then use a black felt-tip pen to draw a line down the back of each one.

Try finger painting stripes on some of your bugs instead of spots.

You could add feelers and eyes to your bugs.

Make sure the giftwrap is dry before using it.

You could cut out a bug to make a gift tag.

Apple-print barn owl

Make the body about twice as long as your hand.

Rinse your spoon after spreading each paint, so they don't mix together.

The stalk of the apple should be at the top.

1. Rip a big oval body out of brown paper. Then rip a piece out of the top to leave two tufty ears. Glue the body onto a piece of blue paper.

2. Put three paper towels on top of an old newspaper. Pour a little black, white and orange paint on top. Spread the paint out with a spoon.

3. Cut a small apple in half. Dip one half into the white paint. Press it down near the top of the owl's body to make his face.

You can push a fork into the carrot to use as a handle, if you like.

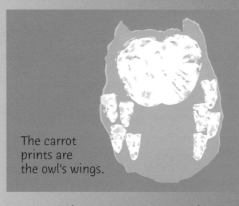

The carrot prints are the owl's wings.

4. Cut the pointed end off a carrot. Then cut the end in half. Dip one half into the white paint. Press it onto the owl's body to print a feather.

5. Dip the carrot into the paint again to print more feathers. Print them on the sides of your owl's body, but leave his tummy bare.

6. Finger paint two big orange eyes. Let them dry. Then finger paint the black middles. Add fingerprints for speckles on the owl's tummy.

7. Dip the clean half of the carrot tip into the orange paint. Press it onto the owl's face to print a beak. Then finger paint some orange toes.

You could add blobs of glitter glue for stars in the sky or use stickers from the sticker pages.

This moon was printed using the thick end of a carrot.

You could give your owl white fingerprints on his tummy as well as black ones.

This owl is sitting on a branch made from ripped paper.

Sam's tissue fish

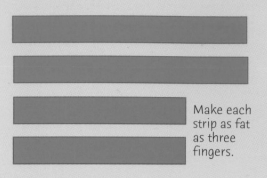

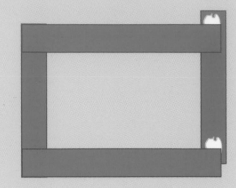

Make each strip as fat as three fingers.

1. Cut two strips of thick blue paper about the length of this page. Then cut two more strips about the width of this page.

2. Spread glue on both ends of one of the short strips. Press the long strips onto it. Glue on the other short strip to make a frame.

3. Put your frame on top of a piece of blue tissue paper and draw around it to make a rectangle. Cut around the rectangle carefully.

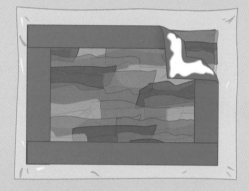

Use an old paintbrush to spread the glue.

Don't make any of the strips longer than your frame.

4. Rip some different shades of blue tissue paper into strips. Lay them on top of a piece of food wrap and spread glue onto them.

5. Lay the rectangle of tissue paper on top of another piece of food wrap. Press the strips onto it, making them go across the paper, like this.

6. Spread glue onto your frame. Then press it on top of the tissue paper rectangle, taking care to line up the edges.

These fish have tails and fins made out of different shades of tissue paper.

You can fill your picture with as many fish as you like. This one has lots of little fish.

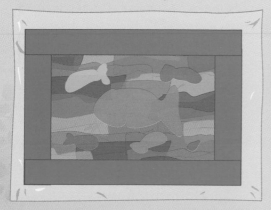

Your outlines don't have to follow the edges of the tissue shapes.

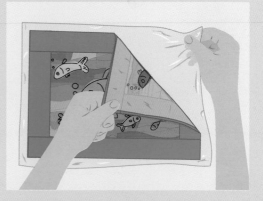

7. Rip some little oval shapes out of bright tissue paper. Spread glue onto them and press them onto the tissue paper in the frame.

8. Leave the picture to dry. Then use a black felt-tip pen to draw fish on top of the tissue shapes. Add little air bubbles from their mouths.

9. Carefully peel your tissue fish picture off the food wrap. Hang it up in a window, so that the light shines through it.

Cut-out farm animals

1. Fold a rectangle of thick white paper about the size of this page in half so that the two shorter edges meet. Press along the fold.

2. Draw a straight line about a finger's width from the bottom. Fold the paper inward along the line. Do the same on the other side.

3. Draw a cow on the folded paper, like this. Make its back go along the top fold and its feet go all the way to the bottom.

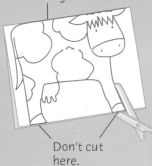

Don't cut along this side.

Don't cut here.

4. Cut out the cow shape, cutting through both sides of the folded paper. Don't cut along its back or the bottom of its feet.

5. Turn the folded paper over and draw the cow on the blank side too. Fill it in on both sides of the paper using felt-tip pens.

6. Cut out a small rectangle of thick green paper. Spread glue onto the folds under the cow's feet and press them onto the green paper.

You can make more animals in the same way, to create your own farmyard.

Poppy and Sam's paper kite

Make sure the fold is on the left, like this.

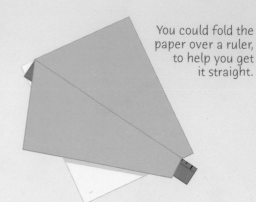

You could fold the paper over a ruler, to help you get it straight.

1. Fold a rectangular piece of fairly thin paper in half so that the two shorter sides meet. Press along the fold.

2. Make a pencil mark two fingers' width from the top left corner. Make another mark the same distance from the bottom right corner.

3. Using a ruler, draw a pencil line joining up the two marks. Then fold the paper along the line, like this. Press it flat.

4. Turn your folded paper over. Then fold the top piece back so that it matches the other side. Press along the fold. Then open it out again.

Fold

5. Lay a ruler on top of the paper from one corner to the other, like this. Draw a dot about 1cm (½in) up from the fold, as shown above.

6. Using a hole puncher or a ballpoint pen, make a hole where the dot is. Make sure the hole goes all the way through the paper.

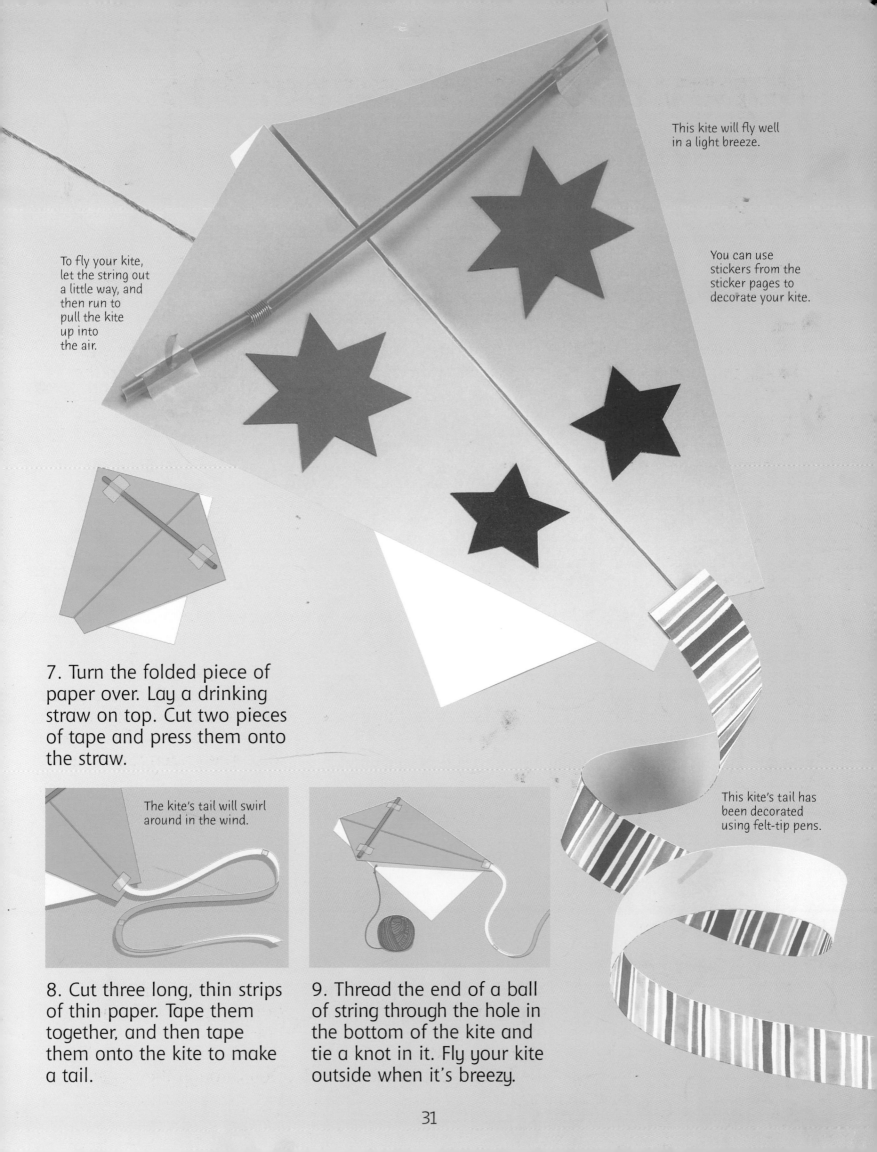

This kite will fly well in a light breeze.

To fly your kite, let the string out a little way, and then run to pull the kite up into the air.

You can use stickers from the sticker pages to decorate your kite.

7. Turn the folded piece of paper over. Lay a drinking straw on top. Cut two pieces of tape and press them onto the straw.

The kite's tail will swirl around in the wind.

This kite's tail has been decorated using felt-tip pens.

8. Cut three long, thin strips of thin paper. Tape them together, and then tape them onto the kite to make a tail.

9. Thread the end of a ball of string through the hole in the bottom of the kite and tie a knot in it. Fly your kite outside when it's breezy.

Mrs. Boot's birthday card

Make the stalks all different heights.

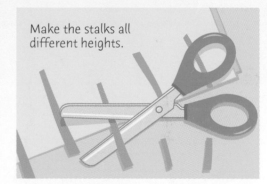

1. To make a long thin card, fold a rectangular piece of thick yellow paper in half so that the two longer edges meet. Press along the fold.

2. Draw seven tulip shapes on bright paper. Cut them out. Then draw seven long stalks on a piece of green paper and cut them out.

3. Glue the stalks onto the card, letting them overlap the bottom edge. Use a pair of scissors to trim the ends off. Glue the tulips onto the stalks.

Edited by Gillian Doherty

Additional illustrations by Erica Harrison, Non Figg, Stella Baggot and Katie Lovell. Photographic manipulation by Nick Wakeford.

First published in 2005 by Usborne Publishing Ltd., 83-85 Saffron Hill, London, EC1N 8RT, England www.usborne.com